Totally AMAZING FACTS ABOUT MILITARY LAND VEHICLES

CARI MEISTER

The Country School

CAPSTONE PRESS
a capstone imprint

USED IN WORLD WAR I (1914–1918), MARK 1 TANKS CAME IN TWO VERSIONS: THE "MALE" AND THE "FEMALE." (THE "MALE" TANK WEIGHED A LITTLE MORE.)

THE TANK WAS LOUD, AND FUMES FROM THE ENGINE OFTEN MADE THE CREW SICK!

It was such a beast of a **machine, it took**

FOUR

men to drive it.

3

The **BUSHMASTER** armored vehicle has **SPECIAL TIRES.** Even if the tires are **PUNCTURED, YOU CAN KEEP DRIVING.**

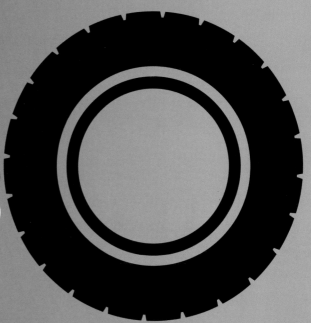

4

It can run for up to **three days** without stopping!

It takes only **ONE PERSON** to drive it. But it has room for up to **NINE MORE PEOPLE.**

5

Need a tow?
THE KETTENKRAD
could tow planes on an airstrip.

This machine was **HALF TANK/HALF MOTORCYCLE!** The Germans used it in World War II (1939–1945).

AFTER THE WAR, FARMERS USED IT AS AN ATV (ALL-TERRAIN VEHICLE).

The RhinoRunner was used to transport soldiers ON DANGEROUS ROADS DURING THE U.S. Iraq War (2003–2011).

This **VEHICLE** has survived 250 pounds (113 kilograms) of **EXPLOSIVES** detonated just 6.5 feet (2 meters) away!

People call it the "toughest bus on the planet."

USED IN WORLD WAR II, NOT MUCH IS KNOWN ABOUT THIS SMALL, ONE-MAN ROLLING TANK.

WHAT WE DO KNOW:

1) IT WAS MADE BY THE NAZIS.

2) THEY SHIPPED IT TO JAPAN.

3) IT WAS NEVER USED ON THE BATTLEFIELD.

The Country School

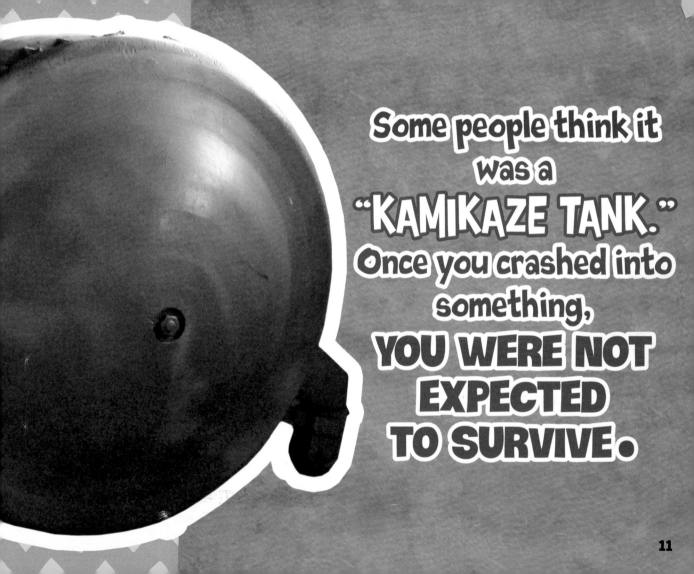

Some people think it was a "KAMIKAZE TANK." Once you crashed into something, YOU WERE NOT EXPECTED TO SURVIVE.

THE GUSTAV WAS THE HEAVIEST MOBILE ARTILLERY EVER BUILT. IT WEIGHED MORE THAN 1,300 TONS (1,180 METRIC TONS)!

The Gustav fired the HEAVIEST SHELLS of its day.

IT TOOK ALMOST **THREE DAYS** TO SET IT UP AND PREP IT FOR FIRING.

13

SOLDIERS PARACHUTED WITH THESE SCOOTERS

INTO ENEMY TERRITORY.

THE SCOOTERS COULD GO AS FAST AS 40 MILES (64 KILOMETERS) PER HOUR!

They could travel through 1 FOOT (0.3 M) of water.

14

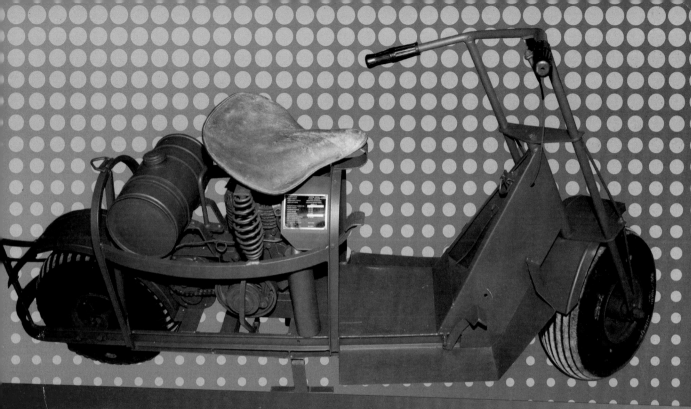

DO YOU WANT A CUSHMAN MODEL 53 SCOOTER? TODAY YOU CAN BUY A REFURBISHED ONE FOR ABOUT **$13,000.**

The Coyote armored vehicle is a high-tech spy machine.
THIS VEHICLE HAS:

radar

infrared

video surveillance

IT CAN DETECT VEHICLES UP TO 15 MILES (24 KM) AWAY.

THE COYOTE IS ONLY ABOUT 21 FEET (6.4 M LONG), BUT IT WEIGHS MORE THAN 14 TONS (12.7 METRIC TONS).

THE AARDVARK IS A MINE-FLAIL VEHICLE. IT CLEARS A PATH OF MINES BY DETONATING THEM.

SPECIAL SOUND-PROOFING IN THE CAB KEEPS THE CREW IN A NEAR-SILENT ENVIRONMENT.

The rear flail has
72 CHAINS
with striker tips.

CREWS ARE SAFE IN THIS BEAST!
No crew member in the vehicle has ever been hurt
when flailing live mines.

Is the mission TOO RISKY for the average soldier? Send in the BLACK KNIGHT!

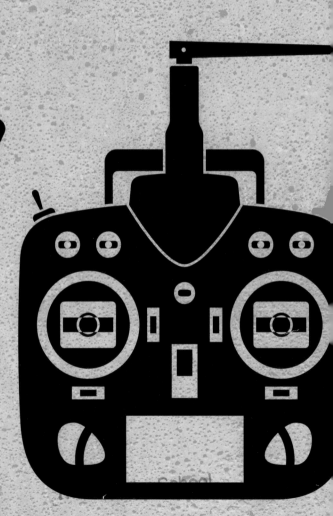

THE BLACK KNIGHT IS A UGCV: UNMANNED GROUND COMBAT VEHICLE.

Think you can hide? Not with this vehicle! It is a spying machine with video and thermal cameras.

SOLDIERS OPERATE IT KIND OF LIKE A REMOTE CONTROL CAR, BUT IT IS MUCH MORE ADVANCED.

During World War I, **RUSSIA** ordered Austin Armoured cars from **BRITAIN.**

THE **SPOKES** OF THE CARS WERE MADE OF **WOOD.**

The crew included a driver, a commander, and two gunners.

THE CAR HAD SMALL SLITS FOR WINDOWS, SO NONE OF THE CREW COULD SEE WELL.

The Vespa 150 TAP was made to be dropped from a plane: a two-person team would parachute with it!

If the machine blew out a tire in **ENEMY TERRITORY,** it had a spare stored in front of the **DRIVER'S SEAT.**

This VESPA could make a SMOKESCREEN to help a driver ESCAPE!

Designed for use in WORLD WAR II, the Weasel worked in SNOW, WATER, AND MUD.

to Berlin

U.S.A.
40185015-S

INSTALL DRAIN PLUGS IN HULL
BEFORE ATTEMPTING TO FLOAT

TWIN RUDDERS whisked the Weasel through **WATER.**

Muddy and wet areas were no match for **THE WEASEL!**

ASTROS can fire up to FIVE DIFFERENT KINDS of ROCKETS.

Unlike other vehicles of its kind, it can fire JET-POWERED CRUISE MISSILES.

AT 55 miles (88.5 km) per hour, THE ASTRO IS NO TURTLE IN THE FIELD!

THEY ARE SOMETIMES PUT ALONG THE COAST TO ACT AS A DEFENSE SYSTEM.

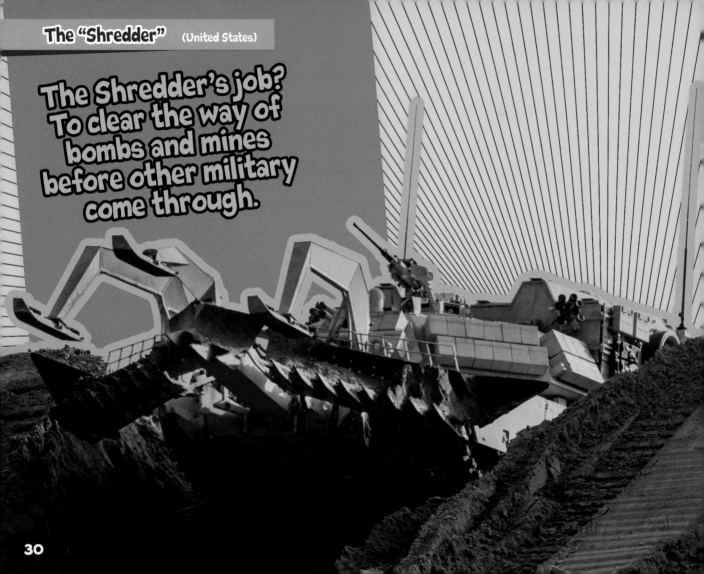

The "Shredder" (United States)

The Shredder's job? To clear the way of bombs and mines before other military come through.

THE SHREDDER WEIGHS **72 TONS** (65 METRIC TONS)! That's about as much as **36 CARS!**

ITS 3-TON PLOW is 15-feet (4.6-m) wide: the plow alone weighs as much as **THREE ASIAN ELEPHANTS!**

If you like remote control cars, **YOU'LL LOVE THE SHREDDER.** It can be run via remote control.

The DD TANK was nicknamed the "DONALD DUCK TANK" because it could operate in water.

IT COULD GO 21 MILES (34 KM) PER HOUR ON LAND

AND

4 KNOTS (ABOUT 4.6 MPH OR 7.4 KPH) AT SEA.

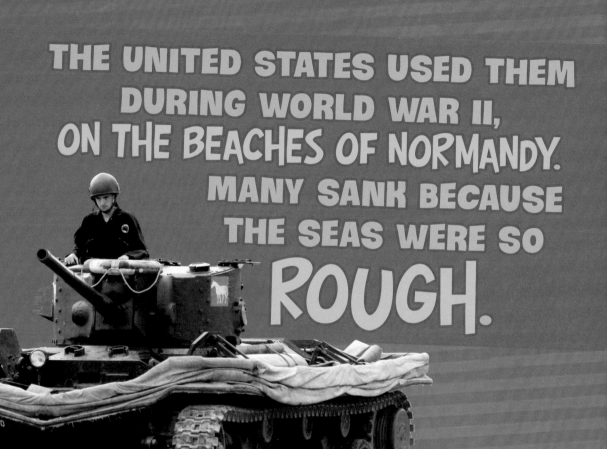

THE UNITED STATES USED THEM DURING WORLD WAR II, ON THE BEACHES OF NORMANDY. MANY SANK BECAUSE THE SEAS WERE SO **ROUGH.**

33

BMW
made more than
36,000
R12 motorcycles
for the
GERMAN ARMY
in World War II.

THESE MOTORCYCLES WERE USED MOSTLY FOR SPYING AND DELIVERING NEWS AND MESSAGES.

YOU COULD ATTACH A SIDECAR AND A MACHINE GUN TO THEM TOO.

They were a **FAVORITE** on the front lines because of their **SPEED** and **MANEUVERABILITY.**

FACE OFF:

MODERN DAY ANTI-AIRCRAFT VEHICLES

COUNTRY:

YEAR IN SERVICE:

MAXIMUM SPEED (MPH/KPH):

FIREPOWER:

KTO ROSOMAK

Poland

2003

62 mph (100 kph)
1 autocannon
1 machine gun
6 smoke grenade dischargers

NORINCO TYPE 95

China

1999

34 mph (55 kph)
4 autocannons
8 smoke grenade dischargers

The SCORPION is like a PUMPED-UP DUNE BUGGY.

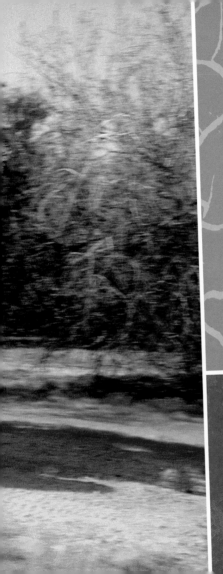

Navy SEALS and other soldiers have **ZIPPED** around in the Scorpion during desert wars.

IT CAN GO 200 MILES (322 KM) WITHOUT REFUELING.

Zaamurets was an armored **MILITARY TRAIN** built in Russia in 1916.

IT HAD TWO GUN TURRETS THAT COULD **SPIN ALL THE WAY AROUND** AND EIGHT MACHINE GUNS.

It weighed 130 tons (118 metric tons). That's as heavy as 60 CARS!

The Country Schoo

IT WAS SO **MASSIVE,** IT WAS CONSIDERED THE "KING OF THE MECHANICAL BEASTS."

THIS ARMORED CAR'S STRANGE ANGLES SHIELDED RIDERS FROM FLYING BULLETS.

The first **version** of these cars had **THREE TURRETS** for shooting at enemies.

TO AIM THE GUNS, A COMMANDER WOULD HAVE TO HAND CRANK SPECIAL WHEELS TO ROTATE THE TURRETS.

43

MLRS =
Multiple Launch Rocket System

The United States, France, Italy, West Germany, and the United Kingdom were all involved in its development.

Its ballistic missiles can hit targets **186 MILES (300 KM)** away. That's about as far as **WASHINGTON, D.C.** to **TRENTON, NJ!**

IT CAN FIRE 12 ROUNDS OF ROCKETS IN 40 SECONDS!

YOU DECIDE: MAKING PROGRESS?
TANKS THEN AND NOW

Early U.S. Tank:
The Ford Model M1918 Light Tank (1918)

Modern U.S. Tank:
The M1A1 Abrams

WEIGHT:
Ford: 3.3 tons (3 metric tons)
Abrams: 68 tons (62 metric tons)
(about 23 times heavier than the Ford tank!)

RANGE:
Ford: 34 miles (55 km)
Abrams: 265 miles (426 km)
(almost eight times farther than the Ford tank!)

MAXIMUM SPEED:
Ford: 8 mph (13 kph)
Abrams: 42 mph (68 kph)
(more than five times as fast as the Ford!)

VERDICT: PROGRESS MADE

NEED TO DIG A TRENCH FAST? THE BTM-3 CAN DIG AN 800-METER (about a half-mile) TRENCH IN **ONE HOUR!**

IT ONLY TAKES 10 MINUTES TO GO FROM DRIVE MODE TO DIGGING MODE.

WHY WOULD YOU NEED A TRENCH? FOR UNDERCOVER COMMUNICATION OR DEFENSE.

Check out this remote-controlled surveillance and reconnaissance tool —the MAARS.

SEVEN
DIFFERENT KINDS OF SURVEILLANCE CAMERAS ARE PERCHED ON THIS ROBOT.

The Country School

Besides spying, the MAARS can SET EXPLOSIVES, OPEN DOORS, and REMOVE UNWANTED OBJECTS with a special "claw."

Although the MAARS is totally high-tech, IT'S SUPER SLOW. Its maximum speed is 7 miles (11 km) per hour.

"THE THING" was a small, light tank built for the Vietnam War. Its goal: to blow up other tanks.

THE THING was only 12.5 feet (4 m) long by 8.5 feet (2 m) wide. THAT'S ABOUT THE LENGTH OF A MINI COOPER!

STILL, IT SOMEHOW COULD SQUISH THREE CREW MEMBERS INSIDE.

The STORMER is used for many combat duties, INCLUDING SETTING UP MINES.

IT TEARS UP THE ROAD AT 50 MILES (80 KM) PER HOUR.

ON WATER, IT MOVES AT ABOUT 3.1 MILES (5 KM) PER HOUR.

THE PROGVEV-T WAS A SOVIET-ERA TANK WITH A JET FIGHTER ENGINE ATTACHED.

The role of the jet engine: to blast away mines with its

HEAT.

ITS PROBLEM?
IT WAS
VERY HEAVY,
VERY SLOW,
AND
VERY LOUD
(NOT TOO STEALTHY)!

The GOLIATH, made for World War II, was one of the first REMOTE-CONTROLLED BATTLE VEHICLES.

IT COULD CARRY MORE THAN 200 POUNDS (91 KG) OF EXPLOSIVES INTO BATTLE.

58

Think you'd be safe from it while hiding in a trench? Forget about it! **THE GOLIATH COULD SCALE WALLS OF TRENCHES.**

The South African-designed RG-33 MRAP first went into service in 2007.

IT COMES IN BOTH **4X4** AND **6X6** VERSIONS.

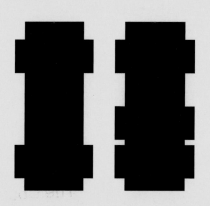

It can be used as an ambulance or a convoy escort.

It can also remove **EXPLOSIVES.**

THE TSAR TANK OF WORLD WAR I LOOKED LIKE A GIGANTIC TRICYCLE.

It was one of the

BIGGEST TANKS

ever made. Its front wheels alone were 27 feet (8 m) in diameter! That's as long as four and a half grown men stacked END TO END!

During the tank's trial runs in 1915 it got stuck in the mud and no one could get it out.

It remained stuck in the mud for eight years until it was taken apart for scrap metal.

The United States made the Boarhound for the British Army to use in World War II.

THE BOARHOUND WAS A LARGE ARMORED CAR WITH EIGHT WHEELS. UP TO FIVE CREWMEN COULD FIT INSIDE.

THE BOARHOUND WAS MADE TO BE USED IN DESERT ENVIRONMENTS, LIKE NORTH AFRICA, WHERE SPEED AND SKILLFUL MOVEMENT WERE VERY IMPORTANT.

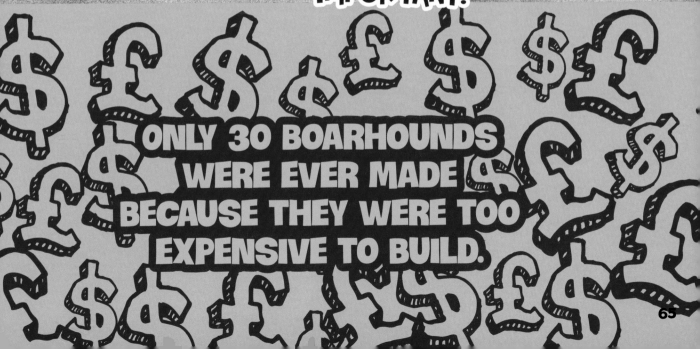

ONLY 30 BOARHOUNDS WERE EVER MADE BECAUSE THEY WERE TOO EXPENSIVE TO BUILD.

Playing tubas during battle? The Japanese War Tubas were built with acoustic locators that looked like tubas.

JAPANESE SOLDIERS MAY HAVE USED THIS MACHINE TO LISTEN FOR ENEMY PLANES DURING WORLD WAR I.

EARLY DETECTION OF ENEMY PLANES MEANT MORE TIME TO PREPARE FOR AN ATTACK.

WATCH OUT!

Unlike some tanks, a Merkava can fire at moving targets while moving.

THE **MERKAVA 4** HAS A THERMAL SHROUD ON THE GUN. THE SHROUD KEEPS THE BARREL FROM OVERHEATING AND

BENDING.

THE SANDCAT IS USED BY SEVEN DIFFERENT COUNTRIES.

Its armor is made from steel and ceramic. The lightweight armor makes it a fast vehicle.

THE SANDCAT CAN BE STOCKED WITH A 40-MM AUTOMATIC GRENADE LAUNCHER, A 7.62 MM MACHINE GUN, OR A 12.7 MM MACHINE GUN.

YOU CAN ARM IT BY REMOTE CONTROL!

THE STRUMTIGER WAS A WORLD WAR II NAZI ROCKET LAUNCHER.

Loading the rocket was so tricky, it took five men to do it.

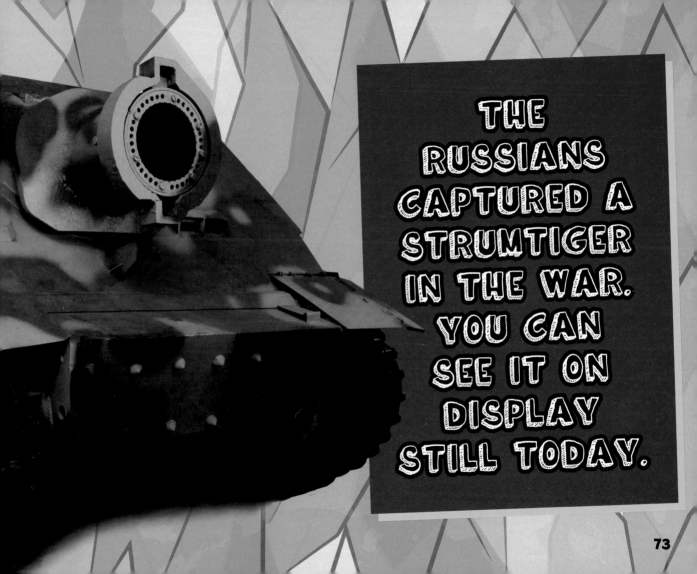

THE RUSSIANS CAPTURED A STRUMTIGER IN THE WAR. YOU CAN SEE IT ON DISPLAY STILL TODAY.

U.S. PARATROOPERS NOW CARRY FOLDABLE BIKES INTO ENEMY LANDS.

The bike can be folded up in 30 seconds.

WHY CARRY A BIKE? SOLDIERS ON BIKE CAN MOVE QUICKLY AND SILENTLY THROUGH ENEMY TERRITORY.

THE PARATROOPER BIKES CAN CARRY UP TO 500 POUNDS (227 KG) OF GEAR.

CHECK OUT
THIS ROUGH-TERRAIN MILITARY ROBOT!

BOSTON DYNAMICS
is working on a
rough-terrain robot called
"BIG DOG"
for the U.S. Army.

BIG DOG IS ABOUT 3 FEET (91 CM) LONG AND 2.5 FEET (76 CM) TALL.

IT CAN RUN AND WALK THROUGH RUBBLE, MUD, SNOW, DIRT, AND WATER.

IT TOOK 10 MEN TO RUN THIS BEAST OF A TANK.

THE FIAT 2000 WAS CALLED THE "PILLBOX" BECAUSE OF ITS BOXY SHAPE.

It was used in WORLD WAR I, but only two were EVER MADE.

The NAMICA missile carrier can carry A WHOPPING EIGHT ready-to-fire missiles.

DON'T BLINK! THIS BAD BOY LAUNCHES FOUR MISSILES IN ONE MINUTE!

The Country

THE MISSILES CAN EVEN BE FIRED IF THE TANK'S ENGINE IS POWERED OFF

THE HMMWV IS SHORT FOR HIGH MOBILITY MULTI-PURPOSE WHEELED VEHICLE. MOST PEOPLE KNOW THIS AS A HUMVEE.

THE HMMWV CAN CONQUER ALL KINDS OF TERRAIN —FROM JUNGLE TO DESERT!

949623

Is the D-9R Dozer a tank or a bulldozer? BOTH!

THE ISRAELI ARMY USES ARMORED BULLDOZERS TO CLEAR AWAY RUBBLE IN **ANTI-TERRORISM OPERATIONS.**

A SOLDIER CAN OPERATE THIS ARMORED BULLDOZER BY REMOTE CONTROL!

IF SEARCHING AND DESTROYING IS THE JOB, THE GLADIATOR HAS IT COVERED!

THIS REMOTE VEHICLE CARRIES MINI-MISSILES AND GRENADE LAUNCHERS.

THE GLADIATOR HASN'T SEEN ANY BATTLE ACTION YET. IT'S STILL BEING DEVELOPED.

CHINESE

THE CHINESE USED WAR CHARIOTS AS EARLY AS **1200 BC.**

THE CHARIOTS WERE USED IN BATTLE, IN ROYAL HUNTS, AND TO MOVE SUPPLIES.

THE HITTITES USED CHARIOTS WITH A DRIVER AND A FIGHTER.

The fighter threw **JAVELINS** or used a **BOW AND ARROW** to thwart enemies.

THE HELEPOLIS WAS ONE OF THE FIRST ARMORED VEHICLES USED FOR FIGHTING.

The HELEPOLIS, used in the Siege of Rhodes, was the largest siege tower of the ancient world: 130 FEET (40 M) TALL and 65 FEET (20 M) WIDE. It was called "THE TAKER OF CITIES."

IT WAS COVERED IN **SEAWEED** AND **ANIMAL SKINS** TO MAKE IT **FIREPROOF.**

The Taker of Cities failed because it got stuck in the mud and couldn't be moved.

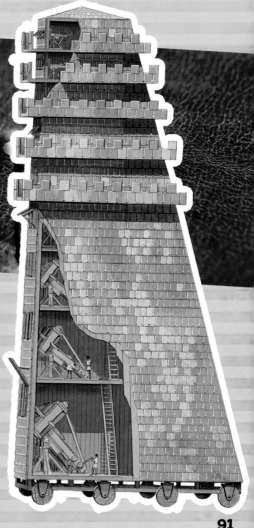

The M3 Stuart was first developed following World War I **MORE THAN 100 YEARS AGO.** But the Paraguay Army **STILL USES IT TODAY!**

IT WAS NAMED AFTER THE U.S. CIVIL WAR CONFEDERATE GENERAL, J.E.B. STUART.

THIS TANK HAS BEEN USED ALL OVER THE WORLD IN MANY DIFFERENT CONFLICTS.

THE 2S35 KOALITSIYA-SV IS A KIND OF HOWITZER. IT'S A LONG-RANGE WEAPON.

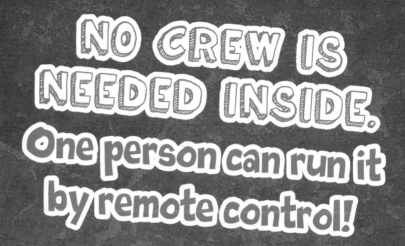

NO CREW IS NEEDED INSIDE. One person can run it by remote control!

It has a higher rate of fire than any other artillery system. **IT CAN FIRE 16 ROUNDS PER MINUTE!**

THE M151 WAS NICKNAMED THE "MUTT" (MILITARY UTILITY TACTICAL TRUCK).

Unlike other military Jeeps, this one was not sold to the public. **IT ROLLED OVER TOO EASILY.**

An Army report claimed that the M151 was involved in **3,538 ACCIDENTS** in the span of one year!

AN EGG-SHAPED "BLAST BUCKET" HOLDS THE ULTRA AP'S CREW UP TOP.

THE BLAST BUCKET PROTECTS SOLDIERS IN CASE OF A ROLLOVER OR ENEMY FIRE.

The Ultra AP is a prototype. It has not seen combat yet.

THE FOX WAS A CANADIAN-DEVELOPED ARMORED VEHICLE. IT WAS USED IN **WORLD WAR II** AND THE PORTUGUESE COLONIAL WAR.

TWO BROWNING MACHINE GUNS PERCHED ON THE FOX.

PARTS OF THE RETIRED FOX WERE RECYCLED AND USED ON ANOTHER COMBAT VEHICLE: THE SABRE TANK.

LOOKING FOR A NEW RIDE? YOU CAN BUY A REFURBISHED FOX TODAY FOR ABOUT $30,000.

THE BEAVERETTE WAS A LIGHT-ARMORED CAR DESIGNED TO DEFEND BRITISH AIRFIELDS.

F/11

RAF7468

Its armor was created from flat sheets of steel.

THE BEAVERETTE HAD TINY WINDOWS. SOME SAY THE DRIVER NEEDED A SECOND GUY TO STICK HIS HEAD OUT THE TOP AND TELL HIM WHERE TO GO.

THE M1249 IS A BEEFED-UP TOW TRUCK.

It can tow disabled vehicles weighing up to **41 TONS (37 METRIC TONS)!**

When a tank breaks down, **THE M1249 COMES TO THE RESCUE.**

ESCORT WAGONS FOR THE... MILITARY?

Wagons towed by horses and mules were common military vehicles during the Civil War (1861–1865).

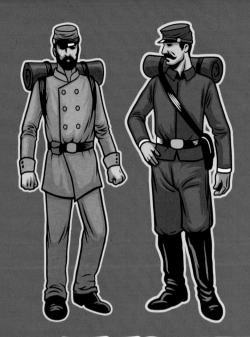

THE WHEELS EACH HAD 16 SPOKES, MAKING THEM VERY STRONG.

THE ESCORT WAGON WAS USED TO TRANSPORT TROOPS.

WHOA!
This is the BIG DADDY!

The T28 was the biggest tank ever made by the United States.

WHEN FULLY LOADED WITH WEAPONS, IT WEIGHED ABOUT 95 TONS (86 METRIC TONS). THAT'S ABOUT THE WEIGHT OF 75 POLAR BEARS!

SOME OF ITS ARMOR WAS 12 INCHES (30 CM) THICK.

BECAUSE OF ITS WEIGHT, THE T28 WAS SUPER SLOW! IT TOPPED OUT AT JUST 8 MILES (13 KM) PER HOUR.

GLOSSARY

acoustic locators—machines that detect the sounds of aircraft

anti-terrorism—the practice, tactics, and strategy military agencies use to fight or prevent terrorism

flail—a mine flail is a tool that clears a safe path through a mine field by setting off the mines on purpose

howitzer—a short gun used to fire shells

infrared—rays of light that cannot be seen

prototype—a first model of something

reconnaissance—a mission where soldiers go to find out details about an enemy

refurbish—to repair

shroud—something used to hide or shield something

siege tower—a type of vehicle built to withstand attack while trying to breach defensive walls

surveillance—the act of keeping very close watch on someone, someplace, or something

thermal camera—a camera that can take pictures in the dark based on the heat signature of objects

torque—a force that makes something rotate

turret—the part on a military vehicle from which guns are fired

READ MORE

Abramovitz, Melissa. *Military Trucks.* North Mankato, Minn.: Capstone Press, 2012.

Kenney, Latchana Karen. *National Geographic Kids Everything World War I: Dig in With Thrilling Photos and Fascinating Facts.* Washington, D.C.: National Geographic, 2014.

Wesley, Jack. *Military Vehicles.* New York: Scholastic, 2014.

INTERNET SITES

FactHound offers a safe, fun way to find Internet sites related to this book. All of the sites on FactHound have been researched by our staff.

Here's all you do:

Visit *www.facthound.com*

Type in this code: 9781515745273

INDEX

Mind Benders are published by Capstone,
1710 Roe Crest Drive, North Mankato, Minnesota 56003
www.mycapstone.com

Editors: Megan Atwood and Megan Peterson
Designer: Kyle Grenz
Media Researcher: Jo Miller
Production Specialist: Tori Abraham

Library of Congress Cataloging-in-Publication Data
Names: Meister, Cari, author.
Title: Totally amazing facts about military land vehicles / by Cari Meister.
Description: North Mankato, Minnesota : Capstone Press, [2017] | Series: Mind
   benders | Includes bibliographical references and index. | Audience: Grades 4–6. |
   Audience: Ages 8–11.
Identifiers: LCCN 2016038566| ISBN 9781515745273 (library binding) |
   ISBN 9781515745297 (paperback) | ISBN 9781515745310 (ebook PDF)
Subjects: LCSH: Vehicles, Military—Juvenile literature.
Classification: LCC UG615 .M45 2017 | DDC 623.74/7—dc23
LC record available at https://lccn.loc.gov/2016038566

Photo Credits
Alamy: Andrew Kitching, 26, Chronicle, 78, Colin C. Hill, 33, CPC Collection, 97, Ian Nellist, 15, INTERFOTO, 35, iWebbstock, 5, Mihai Popa, 70, Sueddeutsche Zeitung Photo, 13; Getty Images: Archive Photos/Buyenlarge/Bain News Service, 41, De Agostini Picture Library, 89 (top left), SSPL/Florilegius, 88, The LIFE Images Collection/Carl Mydans/Contributor, 93, The LIFE Images Collection/Greg Mathieson/Mai, 38; Library of Congress, 92 (inset), 106; Newscom: akg-images/Peter Connolly, 91 (right), EPA/Ali Haider, 8, KRT HANDOUT, 50, WENN/JP5/ZOB/BigDog image courtesy of Boston Dynamics ©2009, 77, Xinhua News Agency/Jia Yuchen, 94; Nova Development Corporation, 22 (flags); Photo by REX: Shutterstock, 19; Shutterstock: aarrows, 14, Arcady, 9, Art tools, 67, Bascar, 64 (bottom), bazzier, 107 (left), bekulnis, 14, BOONROONG, 87, caesart, 34, Carsten Reisinger, 92 (flag), Color Brush, 91 (left), Dxinerz-Pvt-Ltd, 16 (middle), Dxinerz-Pvt-Ltd, 45 (left), Edoma, 6, Everett Historical, 36-37 (background), Fat Jackey, 84, Flik47, 68, Frank Fennema, 107 (right), gdinny, 72-73 (background), Good Vector, 42, i4lcocl2, 55, i4lcocl2, 101, Jaren Jai Wicklund, back cover (bottom left), kontur-vid, 16 (bottom), kontur-vid, 21, Le Do, back cover (right), Leremy, 7, Lilu330, 61, LoopAll, 3 (top), Lukasz Stefanski, 64 (top), Miceking, 51, Mikadun, 7 (background), Mike McDonald, 100, Mr.Creative, 45 (right), Panda Vector, 16, (top), PLRANG ART, 37 (left), RedlineVector, 57, Regular, 32 (background), Robert Spriggs, 43, Roman Sotola, 20, SFerdon, 3 (bottom), stockphoto mania, 22 (wood), Tribalium, 89 (bottom left), Venomous Vector, 4, Voropaev Vasiliy, 31 (right), woverwolf, 89 (bottom right), Yayayoyo, 29; The Image Works/RIA-Novosti, 73; U.S. Army Photo by Capt. Tania Donovan, 83, Sgt. Scott Davis, 104; U.S. Marine Corps Photo by Lance Cpl. Preston McDonald, 30, Lance Cpl. William Hester, cover (top left); U.S. Navy photo by Mr. John F. Williams, cover (top right), 99; Wikimedia, back cover (top left), 66, Ajai Shukla, 81, Alf van Beem, cover (bottom left), 25, Allocer, 12, Articseahorse, 60, Bernhard Gröhl, 11, Chikumaya, 74, DoD photo by: TECH. SGT. H. H. DEFFNER, 28, Janez Novak, Ljubljana, Slovenija, 49, LOC/Bain News Service, 2, Mark Holloway, 108, Max Smith, 37 (right), Max Smith, 102, Mike from Vancouver, Canada, 16, Randen Pederson, cover (bottom right), SSG Richard Hart, 44, The source Unknown, 23, Unknown, 62, US Army, 59, User:J JMesserly, 56, USMC Archives from Quantico, USA, 52

Design Elements by Capstone and Shutterstock

Printed in Canad
010037S